How to Start a Br

ISBN-13: 978-147924{

ISBN-10: 1479248371

Copyright Notice

All Rights Reserved © 2012 Louise Tiptel

HOW TO START A
BRIDAL SHOP BUSINESS

Louise Tiptel

I dedicate this book to everone– who has been lucky enough to have their lives touched by the joy, pleasure and sheer excitement of bridal shopping...

Contents

Starting a Bridal Shop Business: An Overview

There are millions of weddings being conducted each year, with each wedding costing an average of $26,000!

This means that weddings have a total market value of about $58 billion.

It's no wonder, then, that magazine shops fill their shelves with rows upon rows of wedding magazines.

It is, after all, a very lucrative business to be in. And it's an industry you can easily enter and profit from as well.

If you naturally love assisting brides-to-be in making sure that everything goes perfectly well on their big day, then starting your own bridal shop business may be something you'd want to look into.

Who knows, this just might be the perfect business venture for you.

Take note that most of the existing bridal shops typically offer a wide selection of bridal gowns.

To set your own bridal shop business apart and be competitive in the industry, it's a good idea for you to focus on a specific niche.

For example, you can target plus-sized women as your primary clientele.

Another good option would be to offer potential clients a one-stop shop experience.

This means your shop will allow brides-to-be to shop not only for their wedding dress, but also for their shoes, jewellery, purse, and even lingerie.

And you can move your service up a notch by offering free personal consultation as regards each client's choice of gown and accessories to make sure everything coordinates well with everything else.

You can also keep business costs down by opening your shop to a year-round bridal expo.

This involves allowing other local companies engaged in the bridal business to sub-lease a specific area within your bridal shop where they can offer specialized services.

Wedding invitation makers, party favour suppliers, photography and video services providers, catering services, music providers, and honeymoon planners are just some of the businesses you can invite to join your expo.

If you don't have enough room in your shop to sub-lease, then a good option would be to make referral arrangements with these businesses where you get either a percentage or a flat fee for every sale they get as a result of a referral from you and vice versa.

Where to Find Clients

For obvious reasons, it's important for you to know where you can find your prospective clients and where the best place to transact business with them is.

If the parents of the bride are footing the bill, then there's a good chance they spend much of their leisure time in the best country club in town.

It's therefore a good idea to build a strong relationship with the general manager of such establishments, as they can help you catch the attention of your affluent prospects.

It would also be wise to find out where your prospect might go to find a wedding planner or whom they may ask for advice.

If they ask their club manager, then you're already a step ahead. If they simply look for information online, then you'll have to make your presence felt on the internet.

How to Communicate with Prospects

Of course, it's not enough that you know where to find potential clients; you'll also need to learn how to communicate with them properly. Take some time to observe your prospects so you'll know what the best approach is going to be.

Do your target clients simply want a stress-free wedding day?

Are they looking forward to an extravagant fairy-tale celebration?

Do they want their money to be spent wisely and efficiently?

Be sure to approach them with what they want to hear. If you pitch "saving money on a wedding" when what they really want to hear is that you can carry out a grandiose dream wedding, you've already lost the sale at the outset.

When and How to Reach Prospects

Establishing contact and building a relationship with your prospects early gives you the advantage of having less competition.

And if you could build a strong professional relationship with the best jewellers in your area, you just might be able to connect with brides-to-be from the start.

Other professionals you'd want to establish a strong partnership with are wedding photographers.

Newly-engaged couples are likely to get pre-nuptial photos taken and it's a good bet that the photographer they hire for these photos will be the same one they hire for the wedding itself.

Photographers, therefore, often have valuable leads that can help you win a client, which is why it's definitely a good idea to build mutually-beneficial relationships with the best photographers in your area.

Stock

It can be quite expensive to stock your shop with several different bridal gowns of varying sizes, styles, and designs.

Fortunately, there are many bridal gown manufacturers that offer free samples not only of bridal gowns, but also bridesmaids' dresses.

You can use these samples to let clients get a feel of the fabric and see how a dress drapes on her figure.

Regardless of how a sample fits on a client, it should give her a general idea of how the final dress will look on her, which helps in making the final choice.

Become an industry expert

Many of the bridal consultants operating today started out working in some aspect of the entire wedding industry – flower shops, bridal shops, and reception venues – before they finally set out to become a bridal consultant.

This helps ensure that they have considerable first-hand knowledge on the ins and outs of the industry.

Regardless of whether you're seasoned in the business or are a relative newbie, it's important for you to know which vendors are the best in your area.

Once you've identified these vendors, you need to start building relationships with them by visiting their businesses and becoming familiar with it. You should then establish a network of the vendors you trust most.

Take note that the more business you send to a particular vendor, the better their services to you will be. Make sure you have a database of wedding-related providers so you can provide your clients with a variety of options.

Familiarise yourself with the latest wedding trends, ideas, and etiquette

Check out websites, read magazines, and attend bridal events to keep yourself updated and to make sure you always have something fresh to offer your customers.

It may even be a good idea to attend weddings planned by other people so you'll get fresh ideas. This is also a good strategy for identifying mistakes and pitfalls you can avoid or overcome when working on your own wedding projects.

Develop excellent people skills

Take note that the job of a bridal consultant necessarily involves dealing with different individuals and attending to hundreds of details.

People planning a wedding naturally experience a variety of emotions in trying to pull off the perfect wedding celebration.

This is why it's important for you to have excellent skills in dealing with people, navigating through potential pitfalls, and offering practical and effective solutions to sudden problems.

To put it simply, you need the ability to work well under pressure.

Learn how to effectively manage your money

An average wedding typically costs about $20,000 these days, so it's definitely important for a bridal business owner to have the ability to help the bride (or whoever's footing the bill) manage and stretch her budget.

Of course, you should also use your financial management skills to ensure the survival and growth of your business.

Plan your income and set your service rates

Most wedding consultants make their profit by taking 10% to 15% of the wedding budget, but there are also those who operate on hourly rates.

If you're considering going this route, then it pays to take note that an average wedding will require about 75 hours of coordinating.

Remember as well that this type of business is seasonal and you're likely to earn your main income between the months of May and October. You may want to think about offering other events planning services during the months when your wedding business is slow.

Build your portfolio

Ask for letters of reference from your previous clients and obtain their permission for you to use their photos for promotional purposes.

You may then compile these letters and photos, along with a short description of the decisions made and why they were the right decisions under the circumstances.

This portfolio will prove your expertise to new clients at the same time.

A bridal shop business can indeed be a very exciting and rewarding business venture.

As the business owner, you'll get the wonderful opportunity of helping women find the bridal gown of their dreams, and the best thing is that you get paid for doing so.

Regardless of the type of bridal shop you decide to operate or the niche you choose, it will surely be very rewarding to run a business that celebrates love and commitment.

Opening your very own bridal shop can be a lot of fun, very exciting, and extremely rewarding.

Of course, it involves a bit of hard work as well.

So, if you're planning to start your own bridal shop business, then you may want to follow the guidelines laid out below.

These can help minimize your risk and get your business generating revenue as early as possible.

1.   Prepare a business plan

This is perhaps the most important step in getting your business venture off to a good start.

You're probably going to need financing for your business and lending institutions aren't likely to consider a loan application unless you have a good business plan in hand.

Furthermore, the entire process of preparing a business plan allows you to consider every single aspect of starting a bridal shop business, thus ensuring the success of your venture even more.

2.   Choose a name for your business

Make sure the name you choose is catchy and has good recall.

Of course, it should also be a name that tells potential clients immediately what your business is all about.

The name should also be simple enough so it can fit easily into a web address.

The internet, after all, can be among your most powerful advertising tools.

As soon as you choose a name, get it registered with your state and then immediately register the domain name as well.

It may be a good idea to get the domain name with different extensions (.com, .org, .biz, etc.) so competitors cannot register the same name with a different extension.

3. Incorporate your business

This allows you to enjoy limited liability.

Take note that if you decide to be a sole proprietor, you'll have to assume all of the liability for your company.

However, if you incorporate your business, you become a shareholder and therefore can't be held responsible for company debts.

Your individual liability is limited to the amount that you invested in the business.

In this day and age, it's definitely wise to protect yourself against litigation and separate personal assets from company assets.

4. Study the competition

Potential clients are likely to review the services and rates of a few different bridal shops, so you should study your competitors as well.

Based on what you find out about them, determine your own strengths and weaknesses, and then take the necessary measures to reduce your weaknesses and emphasize your strengths.

Make sure that when potential clients compare your business with others in the area, you can offer them something they'll find very difficult to refuse.

5.   Calculate your fees

Take note that you'll need to take into consideration not only inventory costs, but also overhead, labour, and profit.

Remember as well that you'll need to pay take care of self-employment taxes and insurance, among other things.

Be sure to set competitive prices, or be prepared to justify why you charge higher rates than your competitors.

Clients aren't always looking for the cheapest bridal shops, but the one that can give them the best value for their money.

You'll want to make sure you're the kind of business they are looking for.

So now we have covered the overview let's get down to specifics.

Naming Your Bridal Shop Business

Choosing a company name can be the most fun part of starting a company. It can also be one of the most important.

After all, having the right bridal shop business name can be a very effective advertising tool. Among other things, it can give prospective customers a general idea of what your company does and what you have to offer.

In the same way, choosing the wrong name is likely to drive would-be customers away.

Here are a couple of things to remember when choosing a bridal shop business name:

Keep it short and memorable

Needless to say, a short company name is much easier to remember than a lengthy one.

Choosing a short name doesn't just involve using less words, but also words with less syllables.

But, aside from being short, your bridal shop business name also has to be catchy so as to promote better name recall.

You are your name

This means your company name should reflect the company's personality.

It should give people a general idea of what services you provide or what benefits they can get from patronizing your bridal shop business. You need to have an image which you want your bridal shop business to project and the name you choose must fit that image.

More importantly, you have to choose a name your target customers can easily connect with. Now, you know the basics of choosing a company name and you realize how important a name is to your business.

However, you shouldn't take the process of choosing a name too seriously. While the company name does have to reflect its personality, it doesn't really have to define your company completely.

Take note that venturing into other related businesses is a normal part of any company's growth, so there is a real possibility that you may have to change your bridal shop business name from time to time.

Again, the name of your bridal shop business is important, but you shouldn't get hung up on the process of choosing it.

As long as you make sure that it's memorable, it tells people what your bridal shop business is about, and you're proud of it, then you're good to go.

Drawing Up a Business Plan

Developing a new bridal shop business naturally requires a good foundation, and building such a foundation begins with having a sound business plan.

Remember that the business plan is an essential part of documenting a start-up business' financial goals, business objectives, and marketing plans.

Implementation of all your bridal shop business ideas can only successfully begin once you've completed your business plan.

Choosing the Right Format

You probably already know that a business plan ranks among the most vital components of starting your bridal shop business and ensuring its success.

But, how exactly do you make a good business plan?

Well, there are several variations and templates you can choose from.

What's important is for you to choose the one that's best suited to the kind of enterprise you'll be running and to the purpose for which you're making the plan in the first place.

Here are some of the things you need to take into consideration:

1. Your Target Audience

There are two types of business plan.

a. There are business plans intended for an internal audience and these plans are usually part of your bridal shop business growth strategy; they're also usually referred to as strategic plans.

b. There are also plans meant for external audiences and the purpose of these plans is usually to attract financing, suppliers, or talent for your bridal shop business.

If the purpose of your business plan is primarily to get funding, then the document will typically be in condensed form, or a sort of summary of a more comprehensive business plan.

Such a version is generally known as a *funding proposal* or a *business opportunity document* and it's usually followed by the larger plan.

A business plan can indeed be a very useful document, so it's important to clearly define the audience for which it is intended.

2. What Goes Into the Plan?

Remember that a business plan needs to be comprehensive and that it's essentially created to put into writing what you envision for your bridal shop business venture.

Your bridal shop business plan should contain:

- An executive summary,
- The background and history of your company,
- A clear description of your bridal shop business concept,
- Your marketing analysis and development plan,
- Your operations and production assessment,
- Your financial assessments and projections,
- Your human resources management assessment and plan,
- Your business implementation plan,
- An identification of resources,

- The proposed investor deal structures wherever appropriate,
- A survival strategy that describes potential risks and mitigation measures,
- Your bridal shop business growth strategy,
- Your exit strategy,
- Appendices.

If that seems daunting, don't worry. Some of the components of your business plan may be longer than others and some of them are optional, depending on your target audience, the format you choose to adopt, and the purpose of your plan.

What's important is for your intended reader to clearly grasp the value proposition, understand why your bridal shop business is expected to succeed, and how that success will be achieved.

If you're pitching the plan to potential investors, (or most probably the bank) then they should quickly understand your proposed deal structure and the possible returns.

3. What Length To Make Your Plan

The average business plan typically consists of 20 pages, though there are some that contain a hundred pages or more.

The length of your plan will depend largely on its purpose and your target audience.

If the primary purpose of your business plan is to attract investors, then you can expect it to contain more details and therefore be lengthier than a plan that's primarily for communicating your bridal shop business growth strategy.

In the same way, the business plan for a venture with a relatively simple concept should be a lot more concise than one that's made for a highly complicated enterprise.

4. Should You Use a Template or Pay a Consultant?

Many people are also confused as to whether they should hire a consultant to help them write their business plan or simply use a template for guidance.

Well, it can be quite tempting to use a template or get someone else to make the plan for you.

However, it's still best if you write the plan yourself even if you do decide to get some guidance from a consultant. After all, who knows your business better than you?

A solid business plan is perhaps the easiest way for you to communicate your bridal shop business ideas to your target audience as well as to help you prevent problems and identify business growth strategies.

It can also be your most valuable tool when you're in search of funding for your bridal shop business.

Remember, though, that instead of treating it as a blueprint or a strict manual which you should implement to the letter, the plan should be seen as more of a guide in operating your bridal shop business.

TIP: Even if you don't have an immediate audience for your plan, the document and even the process itself will definitely prove to be of value to your business in the long run.

Preparing a solid business plan for all the right reasons can indeed increase your chances of attaining success in your bridal shop business.

How to Write the Executive Summary

The executive summary generally serves as the introduction to your formal and comprehensive business plan.

You could even say that this is Part 1 of your business plan.

It contains a summary of your bridal shop business proposition, present business status, financial projections, and the key elements for success.

Although it's often tempting to just rush through this component of your business plan, always remember that an executive summary is likely to be the very first thing your target investors or banking officials will read in the document.

It basically tells the reader the status of the company currently, and where it's expected to go. Many people aren't likely to read the remainder of the plan if the executive summary doesn't catch their interest, so it's really very important to do this right.

The importance of the executive summary lies in the fact that it tells your reader exactly why you believe your bridal shop business will be a success.

Brevity is the key to a solid executive summary, which generally ranges from half a page to a maximum of two pages. Writing anything longer puts you at risk of losing the reader's attention and appearing unfocused. If you can keep the summary under one page without sacrificing quality, then do so.

Note: Although it serves as the introduction, it's best to write the executive summary after you've completed your business plan. After all, it is basically a shorter version of your plan.

To keep the summary consistent with the plan itself, it should have the following components:

1. Your Mission Statement

Your business plan's executive summary is be the best place for you to express your mission statement. Make sure that statement is concise and explains in as few words as possible the existence of your bridal shop business, its goals, and how you plan to achieve those goals.

In short, it should explain your bridal shop business thrust to the reader.

Remember to keep your mission statement focused and direct, leaving no room for confusion as regards what your bridal shop business venture is all about.

2. What's Your Business Concept?

In describing your bridal shop business concept, you'll need to offer some details about the kind of bridal shop business you'll be running, who your target customers are, and what your competitive advantages are.

You may point out that you're filling a void you've identified in the market, offering better prices for comparable services in the industry, or offering a better service than what's currently available.

3. A Little Background

You may also want to give your reader an idea of when your venture began, who the founders are and what functions they perform, how many employees you have (or plan to hire), and where the bridal shop business is located and if there are any subsidiaries or branches.

A description of your offices and facilities as well as the services your offer would also be a good idea.

4. Your Bridal Shop Business Status and Financial Outlook

You'll also need to give a short description of the current status of your bridal shop business. Explain if your business is still in the conceptualization stage, if you've already started setting it up, or if it's already fully operational and you're simply planning to expand.

You should also mention your expected costs and your financial projections for both the short term and the long term.

This will give potential investors an idea of how much capital you need and if your business venture matches the kind of opportunity they're currently looking for. If you already have existing investors, then you'd do well to provide some information on them as well.

5. Key Factors for Success

The reader of your business plan will also appreciate getting a preview of the key factors for bridal shop business success.

These factors depend on your situation, of course, but it generally includes technology patents, strategic partnerships, market factors and economic trends.

If your bridal shop business is already fully operational and you've had some successful projects worth noting (you may have been the first to offer a certain service in the industry), then you should include that as well.

Finally...

All in all, your business plan's executive summary should provide its reader with a quick but insightful glimpse into the plan itself.

It's advisable to highlight everything except the mission statement in bulleted lists. Include all of the important points without revealing too much, since each section is discussed in detail within the plan itself, anyway.

More importantly, make sure the summary sells the proposal on its own as much as possible, just in case reader doesn't read your plan. It does happen!

Note: It's also a good idea to draw up a table of contents right after the executive summary so the reader will know where he can find each section in the plan itself.

If you're still in the process of setting up your bridal shop business, then you likely won't have much to write as regards to some of the areas listed above. In that case, focus on your own experience and expertise in the field, and the circumstances that led to your bridal shop business concept.

Tell your target readers how you plan to set your bridal shop business apart from the competition and convince them that there's indeed a need for your business within your target niche or industry.

Company History

After the executive summary, your business plan should contain a section covering your business background or company history. The length of this portion and how it's told will depend largely on how far along your bridal shop business is in terms of operations and development.

Naturally, the business history of a venture that's just starting is totally different from one that's been operating for some time.

It should be about one page long, though it's understandable for a start-up company's history to cover less than an entire page.

What to Include

In this section, you should be able to illustrate how the various elements of your bridal shop business venture fit together and form one successful enterprise.

You should also include some background information on the nature of the bridal shop business itself and identify the factors that are expected to facilitate its success.

Furthermore, don't forget to mention the specific market needs you're planning to satisfy and the ways and methods in which you expect to satisfy these needs.

If possible, you should also identify the specific individuals or groups of people whom you believe have those needs.

An example of a specific market could be:

Women aged 18 to 30 with an income of $80,000 within 50 miles of your location.

How It All Started

Among the things you should include in the company history portion of your business plan is the origin of your bridal shop business concept.

This explains how you first came upon the idea for your bridal shop business and why you decided to pursue that idea. You should also indicate the progress you've made so far as regards operating and growing your business venture. If you're still in the process of starting your business, then say so.

NOTE: It's also a good idea to mention the problems you've encountered along the way and how you handled each of them.

Potential investors and business partners will surely appreciate knowing that they're dealing with someone who's not afraid to deal with challenges from time to time.

Projected Short-Term Growth

You would also do well to include your short-term business growth plans in this section, so the reader will know that you've thought about your venture carefully and that you have concrete plans for its growth.

NOTE: If you're just starting a new bridal shop business, then you may want to include a bit of personal history along with your background.

Among the things you can include are your educational history, technical skills, areas of expertise, relevant professional club memberships, and other bridal shop businesses you may have started or companies you worked for.

TIP: You may even want to share your areas of inexperience or weaknesses and how you intend to compensate for these areas.

Your target investors would definitely appreciate knowing that you're aware of the things you need to improve on and are making concrete efforts at improving them.

Finally...

In summary, the company history section of
your business plan should provide an interested
reader with a much better idea of how your
bridal shop business came to be and who you
are as a businessperson. Again, the key is to
keep this section concise and avoiding unwanted
information.

Organization and Management

This section of your plan includes the following:

- Your company's organizational structure

- The profiles of your management team

- Details about company ownership

- The board of director's qualifications

It's important for you to answer the question of
who does what when you prepare this section.

Explain what each person's background and
qualifications are.

Tell your reader exactly why you've brought or are bringing these people into your organization and management team.

What exactly are they responsible and accountable for? NOTE: You may think this section of the plan is unnecessary if you're setting up a small venture with less than five people on your team, but anybody reading your business plan needs to know who's in charge.

Therefore, you should still provide a description of every department or division, along with their functions, regardless of the size of your company. If there's an advisory board for your business, then you should also identify who's on it and how you plan to keep each member on the board.

- What salary and benefits do you plan to provide for members of your team?

- Will you be offering incentives? If so, what are they?

- How do you plan to handle promotions?

In this section of your business plan, you need to reassure your audience that the people on your team aren't going to be just names on your company letterhead.

What's Your Structure?

One very simple yet effective way of presenting your organizational structure is by creating an organizational chart and then providing a narrative description of the chart.

By doing this, you don't leave anything to chance, you're making sure the functions and responsibilities of each team member has been carefully thought out, and you've ensured that someone's in charge of each and every function in your bridal shop business.

Therefore, no function is taken for granted and there'll be no overlapping of responsibilities.

TIP: Remember that this kind of assurance is very important to your reader, especially if that reader is a potential investor.

Management Profiles

Ask any business expert and he'll probably tell you that among the most significant success factors in any business is the track record and ability of the management team.

This is why it's important for you to provide your reader with a background of the key members of the management team.

Specifically, you'd do well to provide resumes that indicate the name, position and the corresponding functions, primary responsibilities and level of authority, educational background, skills and experience, number of years on your team (unless it's a start-up company), compensation level and basis, previous employment and track record, industry recognitions received, and community involvement.

TIP: When you indicate the track record of your team, be sure to quantify their achievements.

For example, instead of saying:

"Extensive experience in managing a sales department"

you could say:

"Successfully managed a sales department of ten people for 15 years."

It's also a good idea to highlight how the key members of the management team complement your own experience and expertise.

If you're starting a new bridal shop business, then show your reader how the unique experiences of each member of your team can contribute to your business venture's overall success.

Company Ownership

Aside from the organizational structure, this section of the plan should also describe the legal structure and provide important ownership information regarding your bridal shop business.

- Has the business been incorporated? If so, then is it an S or a C corporation?

- Is your business a partnership?

- If so, then is it a limited or general partnership?

- Or are you the sole proprietor of your bridal shop business?

The most important pieces of information you should include in this section are the owner/s' names, ownership percentage, form of ownership, degree of involvement of each owner within the business, common stock, and outstanding equity equivalents.

Board Qualifications

Take note that there's a huge advantage to setting up an unpaid board of advisors for your company, as it can provide you with the kind of expertise the company is otherwise unable to afford. Simply by enlisting the help of some successful businessmen who are popular in the industry and including them in your advisory board, you'll definitely go far in enhancing the credibility of your company and encouraging a perception of expertise.

If the company has a board of directors, then you need to provide the names of the board members, their respective positions in the BOD, their background, the extent of their involvement with the bridal shop business, and their expected contribution to its success.

Your Business Plan – Market Analysis

You may be a hundred percent confident about the quality of the service your bridal shop business has to offer, but unless you're able to connect with your target customers, quality won't do you much good.

You'll have to get your service into your customers' hands, so to speak, to get the necessary sales.

And that's why you need market analysis. This section of your business plan should be used to illustrate your knowledge of the industry. You may also use it to present highlights and conclusions from the marketing research data you've collected.

For your analysis to be reliable, you need to study the three Cs of marketing:

1. Company

2. Customer

3. Competition

Of course, it's understandable that you should be aware of your company's strengths and weaknesses, but you should also know the same things about your competitors so you'll get a better idea of how to deal with them.

More importantly, you need to know who your customers are and what their needs and wants really are.

When you prepare the company analysis component of this section, you'll need to describe the primary industry to which your business belongs, the industry's current size and historic growth rate, the industry's characteristics and trends, and the industry's major customer groups.

All these will put into perspective the description you'll provide of the company you've established or are planning to establish.

Who Are Your Target Customers?

In choosing and defining your target customers, make sure that you narrow it down to a size that you're sure you can manage.

Many business owners make the mistake of trying to provide everything to everybody at once. Slow and sure is often a better philosophy where your business is concerned.

This section of your plan should include information that identifies the unique characteristics of your target customers including:

- Their needs

- The extent to which these needs are being met

- Demographics.

It's also a good idea to identify your target market's geographic location, who among them makes the major decisions, and any market trends that may affect your business.

The size of your target market should also be indicated in this section, along with your expected market share gains and the reason for these expected gains.

You should also indicate your pricing schedule as well as your gross margin targets and whatever discount structures you may be planning.

You'd also do well to identify what resources you plan to use to get information as regards your target market, the media you'll be using to reach the market, your target market's purchasing cycle, and the socio-economic trends likely to affect your target market.

If all this sounds complicated don't worry, just break down each section and do it one at a time.

Your Competition

Of all the Cs you need to study, your competition may be the toughest, especially if you're new to the industry. The first thing you need to do is study your direct competitors.

If you're planning to operate a bridal shop business in your district, then you're likely to get direct competition from the likes of the larger stores.

So it pays to examine all the possible options on how you can set your bridal shop business apart.

It's important for you to identify your direct competitors according to product or service line and market segment.

You should then assess their weaknesses and strengths, determine the level of importance of your own target market to your competitors, and identify the barriers that may pose a challenge as you enter your target niche.

This may include high investment costs, changing technology, existing patents or trademarks, customer resistance, and a difficulty in finding quality personnel.

You'd also do well to determine the market share of each key competitor and then provide an estimate of the time it'll take for new competitors to enter the niche.

Aside from looking for ways to set yourself apart from the competition, you'll also want to see how your business fits into the marketplace itself.

In doing so, you'll have to consider the strengths and weaknesses of your competitors, the possibility of competitors leaving the marketplace and new ones entering it, the services your competitors are relying on for a majority of their revenue, and effective ways of overcoming possible threats from substitute services.

Developing Your Marketing Strategy

Once all three Cs have been addressed, you should be ready to start developing your marketing program. This basically involves an analysis of what's known as the "four Ps."

They are:

1. Product,

2. Place,

3. Price,

4. Promotion.

Product, of course, refers to what you plan to sell (in this case your bridal shop service) Place refers to where you plan to sell it (office, online, or both).

Price refers to the amount you'll charge for each service you'll be offering.

And Promotion refers to the incentives and other promotional strategies you plan to use in order to get your target market to try your services.

To put it simply, a marketing strategy is your way of drawing in customers, which is indeed very important since customers are essentially the lifeblood of any business venture.

There isn't a single way of approaching a marketing strategy. What's important is for your strategy to be uniquely applicable to your bridal shop business and part of a continuing evaluation process that aims to facilitate business growth and success.

In conducting a "four Ps" analysis, you'll likely conduct some market tests and you'd do well to include the results of these tests in this section of your business plan.

All other details of the tests may be attached as an appendix.

The information you provide in this section may include the number of customers who participated in the tests, demonstrations or any information provided to the participating customers, the degree of importance of satisfying the needs of your target market, and the percentage of participants who expressed desire to take advantage of your products and/or services.

After creating your marketing strategy, you'll also need to draw up a sales strategy, which outlines the methods you'll be using to actually sell the services you plan to offer.

There are two very important elements of a good sales strategy.

- The first is your sales force strategy, which determines if you'll be employing internal sales personnel or independent representatives.

  You should also identify the number of people you plan to recruit for your company's sales force as well as the recruitment and training strategies you'll be using.

You'd also do well to present the compensation packages you've lined up for your sales personnel.

- The second element of a sales strategy is a description of the sales activities you've lined up for the company.

A sales strategy is made more manageable when broken down into activities.

For example, you could start with identifying prospective customers and then prioritizing your prospects according to those who have the highest potential of buying your products. From this outline of activities, you can easily determine the number of prospects you may have to get to make a sale and the average amount you'll likely earn from each sale.

You'll also need to draw up a solid market development plan in order to make your market analysis work to your advantage. While the information in your development plan is likely to come into play only when your company has been established and operational for at least a few years, potential investors will surely appreciate the fact that you've already envisioned your company's growth and evolution.

Among other things, your development plan should provide answers to the following questions:

- ➤ Is the market for the services you offer currently growing?

- ➤ Are you planning to offer line extensions or new services within your first few years of operations?

- ➤ Does the market development plan you've crafted offer ways of increasing the overall demand for your services within the industry?

- ➤ Are there alternative ways of making your company more competitive?

Remember that the market analysis is a vital part of your business plan and it's likely to take up a large part of the plan itself.

This is why it's necessary to conduct a thorough research on the competition and on the market you're planning to enter.

Finally...

You may have the best service in the market, but without an organized and well-crafted market analysis and development plan, you still won't be able to guarantee success.

You market analysis helps you identify a clear roadmap of how to bring your services to your target customers.

Financial Projections

Making financial projections for a start-up bridal shop business can be described as both science and art.

Investors may want to see you spell out financial forecasts in cold, hard numbers, but it's not really that easy to predict the financial performance of your bridal shop business several years from now, especially if you're still in the process of raising capital.

Simply put, this is the part where you formally request funding from potential investors and you do that by illustrating how much funding you need for start-up as well as within the first five years of operations.

If you already have an existing business and are looking towards expansion, then you may reflect the funding requirements for the expansion itself.

Potential investors are also sure to appreciate some historical data as regards the financial performance of your company, particularly within the last three years or so, depending on how long you've been in business.

If you have any collateral that can possibly be used to secure a loan, then that's worth noting as well.

Difficulty aside, financial projections are requirements for a solid business plan and you'll really have to deal with them if you truly want to catch your prospective investors' attention.

Regardless of whether your business is a start-up or a growing venture, you'll still need to provide historical and/or projected financial data.

Here are a few useful tips:

1. **Don't let spreadsheets intimidate you**

All financial projections necessarily start with spreadsheet software, with Microsoft Excel being the most commonly used; chances are great you already have the software on your computer.

Other than this, there are also some special software packages that can help you with financial projections. These packages often provide flexibility, which allows you to weigh alternate scenarios or change assumptions quickly whenever necessary.

2. **Create short-term projections as well as medium-term projections**

Specifically, your prospective investors should see financial projections for the first year of operations, broken down into monthly projections.

You should also provide a three-year financial projection that's broken down into yearly projections and a five-year financial projection.

TIP: It's advisable, however, to keep your five-year projection separate from your business plan, but readily available in case a potential investor asks to see it.

When you project business growth, be sure to consider the current state of your market, trends in labour and costs, and the possibility of needing additional funding for future expansion.

3. Make sure start-up fees are accounted for

Never forget to include fees for permits, licenses, and equipment in your short-term projections.

You should also keep the difference between variable and fixed costs in mind when making your projections and differentiate between the two wherever necessary. Variable costs are usually placed under the "costs for goods sold" category.

4. Go beyond your income statement

While your income statement is the basic measuring tool by which projected expenses and revenue can be conveyed, a solid financial projection will go beyond that to include projected balance sheets that show a breakdown of your assets, liabilities, and equity, among other things.

You'd also do well to include cash flow projections that reveal cash movement through the company within a given period.

Estimates of the amount you plan on borrowing as well as expected interest payments on those loans should also be included.

Furthermore, you should make sure your financial projections are all in accordance to the GAAP.

TIP: If you're new to financial reporting or don't understand the last paragraph, then you may want to consider hiring an accountant to review your projections.

5. **Offer two scenarios only**

Although you need to go beyond the simple income statement, remember that where financial projections are concerned, potential investors really want to see only two scenarios: The best- and worst-case scenarios.

Anything more than those two are superfluous and may just cause unnecessary confusion, so skip it.

Finally...

To sum up, this section should tell potential investors how much money you need now and in the near future, your preferred type of funding and terms, and how you intend to use the funds.

NOTE: Take note that the intended use of the funds is a vital piece of information for potential investors and would-be creditors, which is why you need to explain it in this section.

It's also important to include all pertinent business-related information that can possibly affect the future financial situation of your company.

A trend analysis for your financial statements is also very helpful, especially if you present it with graphs, as this is easier to see.

TIP: Above all, you should strive to make reasonable and clear assumptions.

As previously mentioned, financial forecasting is both a science and an art.

You'll need to make several assumptions, but you'll also have to be realistic when making those assumptions.

Going overboard will likely raise red flags for potential investors, so always make sure your projections are backed up by solid research.

Calculating Your Start-up Costs

What are start-up costs?

These are the expenses you have to deal with before your new bridal shop business can actually begin operations and earn revenue.

The concept of start-up costs is very important in tax law because these costs are not considered as deductible expenses, unlike most of the other business costs. You will, instead, need to amortize these costs over the course of a few months or years.

This means you'll only be able to deduct part of the start-up costs each year.

And you can only determine and take full deduction on your other expenses after you have determined start-up costs.

The first step

The first step in calculating the start-up costs of your business is to gather all of the expense receipts from business-related transactions.

Next, determine the exact date when your bridal shop business opened and then separate the receipts into two piles: one pile for the expenses from before your business opened and another pile for expenses incurred after the opening day.

The next step is to remove all of the receipts for items such as research costs, taxes, and deductible interest from the pile receipts before opening day.

These costs can immediately be deducted. Finally, add together all the remaining receipts belonging to your "before opening date" pile. The sum is your total start-up costs, which have to be amortized.

Amortization is usually set over a period of 18 months, and expenses like hiring and training costs, pre-opening advertising, and travel expenses to meet potential suppliers are usually included in the amortized start-up costs.

How to Obtain
Small Business Grants

When starting a business there can be some huge barriers standing in your way, among the biggest of which are start-up costs and other business-related expenses.

You may be planning to take out a loan for the purpose of starting your bridal shop business. Why don't you consider applying for grants from the government or from private organizations instead?

There are several reasons why grants are better than a loan, the most obvious of which is the fact that grants don't need to be repaid.

How exactly can you obtain a business grant and turn your simple idea into a thriving bridal shop business?

Read on to find out. The Catalog of Federal Domestic Assistance is a good place for you to search for a specific grant you can apply for because it contains a list of all grants available for small bridal shop businesses.

The catalog also indicates what type of business qualifies for a particular grant, so you can immediately determine which grants your bridal shop business is likely to qualify for.

Another option is for you to visit the Small Business Administration's website, which promotes federal grant programs that offer almost $2 billion to small businesses, particularly those focusing on providing technological solutions to existing business issues.

Once you have identified the grant programs you will be applying for, you should start preparing a business plan.

Take note that grant organizations base their approval or rejection of your application on the contents of your bridal shop business plan.

- Your plan should therefore include a statement of purpose that is clearly written and effectively defines the goals of your company.

- A good bridal shop business description, an outline of your short-term and long-term goals, a discussion on planned marketing strategies, and a projected financial analysis should also be part of your plan.

The financial section of your plan is very important because organizations usually measure the worth of a candidate based on how you plan to use the grant money.

You should therefore make sure that your financial analysis and hypothetical budget are both conservative and realistic.

When your bridal shop business plan is complete, it's time to create your actual grant proposal.

If you have previous experience in creating such a proposal, then you can save some money by writing the proposal yourself.

However, if you've never written a grant proposal before, then it would be wise to hire the services of a professional writer.

Make sure your proposal includes schematics, reports, and some basic information on planned projects that are likely to be influenced by the grant funds.

Furthermore, grant reviewers are likely to appreciate such attention to detail, which may be seen as a strong commitment to your product.

In this case, the reviewers will be more likely to approve your applying for grant funds. Complete your grant application by including an updated list of contacts.

This list should start with the contact details of the top-level employees.

It should also include the contact details of individuals who can provide important details on the supplementary materials included in your application.

Make sure that all pertinent information on your bridal shop business and requested files by the grant organization are included in your application.

If your application lacks any of these files, then the grant is likely to be denied or the processing could be very slow. Submit your application only when you're sure that it's complete.

It's also a good idea to have your grant application reviewed by family, friends, and colleagues so grammatical errors can be cleared up and anything you may have overlooked can be pointed out to you.

And as a final review process, you should schedule a reading session together with your staff, so you can correct any identified problems. Above all, you should be patient.

Take note that the process of getting approved for grants may take longer to complete than the process of getting approved for loans.

This is because grant applications are reviewed a number of times and most grant organizations have to go through thousands of applications at a time.

Section 9

Getting Insurance for Your Bridal Shop Business

So, you have an idea for a good bridal shop business venture; you even have the name for your new bridal shop business already.

And you've also proceeded to create a business plan and a proposal for a grant application. What else do you need to do prior to actually operating your bridal shop business?

You will need good insurance.

This is actually one of the most important steps you need to take when starting a bridal shop business.

The good news is that there are lots of great places where you can get good advice on the different types of insurance that you may need for your new bridal shop business.

An insurance agent is probably the best person for you to approach if you're looking for advice on getting insurance for your bridal shop business.

More specifically, you should hire the services of an agent for an insurance company that specializes on bridal shop business insurance rather than a general insurance company.

You have to understand that you'll be dealing with a totally different set of risks and challenges with a business than you would with a car or with your home.

Getting insurance from a company that specializes in bridal shop business insurance assures you that the agent you're dealing with really knows what he's talking about.

You can expect the insurance agent to lay out several different insurance options for you.

These options can range from liability insurance for your bridal shop business to auto insurance.

You may also be offered property insurance as well as loss of business coverage, which protects your interests in case a fire breaks out and you end up without a business to run for a month or so.

It's important for you to ask questions and make sure you understand what each type of insurance covers you for so you can be sure to make an informed decision as to which types of insurance you're going to get.

More often than not, you'll be presented with more insurance options than you can afford.

There's also a possibility that the insurance agent you're consulting will present you with more insurance options than your business actually needs.

This makes it even more important for you to understand what each type of insurance covers. Furthermore, the start of a business is usually a time when you will have to take a few risks by taking out less insurance than your bridal shop business needs.

You'll have to decide how much you can afford to spend for insurance and which type of insurance is the most needed by your bridal shop business.

Once you've determined this, you can leave the other types of insurance for later.

Most bridal shop businesses start only with loss of business coverage, others with liability insurance.

The point is to get only the most important insurance coverage that you can afford for starters. As your company grows, it will become more important for you to protect your bridal shop business' assets.

And the good news is that you may able to afford it at that time.

Aside from the insurance that you have previously identified as a need for your bridal shop business, there may also be other types of insurance that your customers expect you to have.

You can work on getting these additional insurance types when the right time comes.

How to Trademark Your Bridal Shop Business Name and Logo

If you have just put up a new bridal shop business, you should be careful not to stop at choosing a name and logo for it.

You should also make sure that the name and logo you chose is adequately protected. This is especially important if one of your business goals is to create an instantly recognizable brand.

The best way to protect your business name and logo is to have it trademarked.

Take note that a trademark is also used to protect symbols, drawings, and any other character associated with your bridal shop business, much like a patent protects inventions.

The whole process of getting your business name and logo trademarked is a relatively simple one.

However, it often takes several months for your trademark registration to really become official.

Following is a quick guide on how you can protect your business name and logo by getting it trademarked.

1. Choose the name and design the logo for your new bridal shop business.

   You have to make sure, of course, that the name and logo you choose are not yet being used by any other company. More importantly, you need to ensure that such name and logo have not already been trademarked by someone else. You can check the database of the official trademark office to make sure you won't run into any legal problems with your chosen name and logo.

2. Once you have established that your chosen bridal shop business name and logo are not yet trademarked, request for and fill-out the necessary paperwork.

   Once the paperwork has been filled out and submitted to the Patent and Trademark Office, the processing of your application for registration will officially begin.

3. Allow five months for the processing to be completed.

   If five months have passed and you still have not received any notification of your trademark having been filed, you may check on its status.

   Take note, though, that it usually takes between five and seven months for a trademark registration process to be completed.

4. Once you receive notification of your trademark having been filed, obtain a copy of it from the trademark office.

   Take note that you will be asked for your registration number when you make the request for a copy of your trademark certificate.

5. Between the fifth and sixth year of your trademark registration, make sure that an "Affidavit of Use" is filed, so as to prevent other companies from using your trademarked name and logo.

You should remember to file two other affidavits as well before every 10-year period of owning the trademark has passed.

Writing an LLC
Operating Agreement

Limited Liability Corporation, or LLC, is the ideal set-up for start-up companies and small businesses because it requires the business owner to take on only limited liability for the company.

And the good news is that creating an LLC is fairly simple and inexpensive. Take note that the operations of an LLC are governed by the LLC operating agreement.

You'll therefore need to learn how to write your LLC operating agreement.

Here is a step-by-step guide:

1. Gather basic information such as the company name and location as well as the names and physical addresses of the members of your company. You should also note your agent's name.

2. Gather all financial information.

    This includes each member's initial contribution to the company and how much each of them will own in terms of percentage of company interest.

You can choose to have either a single-member or multi-member LLC.
For example, you could choose to initially make a contribution of $100 and own a hundred percent of the company.

What's important is for all company members to be included in your LLC operating agreement.

3. Choose and download a sample agreement.

Of course, you can choose to write your own agreement from scratch, but working from a sample would definitely make the process much easier for you.

While operating agreements aren't really that complex, the language used can be very governmental, and basing your agreement on a sample will help ensure that the language is interpreted correctly.

4. Determine if you need the services of a registered agent.

Take note that there's a slight difference in the LLC laws of each state.

The operating agreement typically has a space that needs to be filled in for the registered agent.

If your state's requirements allow it, you can be the one to fill in this space.

5. Check the "Business Purpose" section of your sample agreement and make sure it includes the statement that indicates your company's purpose as engaging in lawful acts or activities for which an LLC may be formed.

   You should also check the language in the "Term" section. "Indefinitely" is commonly used for the term.
   In the terms of dissolution, "by a majority" is also commonly used.

6. You should also check the language in the "Management" section.

   A majority of small bridal shop businesses are managed by the members as a whole, but you also have the option of getting managers for your bridal shop business, especially if there are active and passive members.

Whatever you decide, make sure your agreement contains the appropriate language as to how your company will operate.

7. Personalize the sample agreement by inserting the data from the notes you took as per Step 1 and Step 2. Be sure to include the necessary signature lines.

8. Print the agreement as well as a list of all members with their respective addresses and then staple them together.

   Let all members sign the agreement, have it photocopied, and then provide each member with a copy.

   Be sure to keep the original somewhere safe and have additional copies in your files for reference.

Take note that this step-by-step guide does not constitute legal advice.

If there's anything about forming an LLC that you don't understand, it's still best to seek the advice of an attorney.

Writing a Company Brochure

A company brochure, also known as a corporate brochure, is an excellent way of introducing your bridal shop business to your target market. That is, of course, if you do it right.

The very first things you need to take into consideration are the logo, font, and color you use on your brochure.

People will only learn about your bridal shop business if they read the brochure, and they are more likely to read a brochure if the cover has an attractive design, which is why your choice of logo, font, and color is very important.

Take note as well that people are more likely to patronize your bridal shop business if you're able to build a connection with them and if you're able to establish in their minds the thought that you can be trusted.

The best way to do this using a brochure is to include pertinent information such as the background and history of your company, what you have to offer, and how you intend to deliver whatever it is you're offering.

You may also include information on how your company intends to serve the community as a whole.

Furthermore, you'll need to provide an explanation of what the brochure itself is all about.

- Is it just about the organization or does it present the products and services as well?

- Is it all about the industry and what role your company plays in its development?

- Is it for a specific event where your company is a participant or is it a detailed brochure of your company?

And of course, you'll have to tell the reader at the outset what the brochure's relevance to him is.

Therefore, before you even start writing your company brochure, you'll first have to think about what you want the brochure to portray and who your target audience is.

You may want to set-up a brainstorming session with your company's key personnel for this purpose.

And take note that even as your brochure contains all the necessary information as discussed above, it should remain concise and easy to read.

You should also make it easy for the reader to select which particular piece of information he wants to read.

This can be achieved through the use of headings and sub-titles.

As long as you keep these tips in mind, you should be able to create a company brochure that truly presents your bridal shop business in a positive light.

Leasing Space

Having enough space for your business is one of the most critical factors in operating a new business as you need retail space to sell your products to potential new customers, so I have covered the basics of acquiring retail space here.

In choosing retail sales space, you'll have to take several things into consideration.

Among these things are good visibility of the location from the street, and easy access for your customers.

You'll also have to decide if you're going to build, buy, or rent your retail sales space.

There are many advantages to renting space as opposed to buying or building. Maintenance, flexibility, and taxes are perhaps the three most important advantages.

Maintenance

If you rent retail sales space, you'll be responsible only for a bit of routine maintenance issues like the replacement of light bulbs, repairing uninsured damages caused by negligence on your part, and cleaning the premises.

The good news for you is that major maintenance issues like electrical, plumbing, air conditioning, heating, and structural problems are the responsibility of your landlord.

This means that if your roof starts to leak, it will be your landlord's responsibility to have it repaired.

Knowing that your rent already covers major maintenance issues makes it so much easier for you to budget your company's available funds.

Flexibility

Renting space helps you avoid being forced to stay at the same location even when it's no longer practical to do so.

Even if you have a lease contract for a specific period, that's still a lot better than getting locked into a commercial mortgage.

If the demographics in your area change, then it will be much easier to relocate your bridal shop business if you're simply leasing or renting space.

This also holds true for the time when your bridal shop business has grown such that you need more space.

Furthermore, you won't have to worry about selling your existing location if you have to move to a new place, which is an issue you'll have to deal with if you own the space.

Taxes

It's very easy to understand the advantages of renting space where taxes are concerned. Rental payments are considered business expenses and are therefore deductible.

On the other hand, only the interest that you pay for commercial mortgages is deductible.

You have to consider as well, the fact that commercial property often doesn't appreciate as much as residential properties, which means your property may accrue very little equity over time.

When you weight this against the 100% deductibility of commercial rent, you'll realize how advantageous it is to simply lease retail space.

Now that you understand the benefits of leasing retail sales space, you'll have to learn how to find the perfect location for your bridal shop business.

Remember that leasing will affect not only your company's profit, but also its ability to grow as well as the satisfaction level of your employees.

So, before you go out looking for space to rent, you'll have to know exactly what you are looking for.

Here's how to identify the perfect retail sales space for your bridal shop business:

1. Determine how much space your bridal shop business needs now and how much it may need in the future. The rule of thumb in determining space requirements is to have 175-250 sq. ft. of space for each person who will be working at the location.

2. Contact a real estate agent and seek advice in finding a suitable commercial space.

Agents typically have the inside scoop on what'd going on in the real estate market and they can advise you properly on which particular properties are ideal for your purposes. It's a good idea to contact a real estate firm that specializes in office space rentals.

3. Discuss any necessary improvements with your potential landlord.

   Take note that improvements are usually subject to serious negotiations, especially if there are lots of vacancies.

   You would also do well to check out the parking space.

   Does the rental offer a number of slots you can set aside for yourself and your employees, or would you have to compete with the public for street parking?

4. You may be able to reduce rental cost by either sharing space or looking out for incubators.

You could share your reception area, rest rooms, and conference rooms with another small firm to reduce your rental costs – that is, if you're okay with having less privacy.

Incubators are small unused areas in a larger building which are usually offered for lease at much lower costs.

These are also good options for a small bridal shop business like yours, provided it meets with your requirements, of course.

5. You may also want to consider renting an all-inclusive suite.

   The rate for executive office suites is usually higher, but they usually come fully-furnished and provide you with access to meeting rooms and office equipment, thus significantly reducing your up-front costs.

   Many of these suites even come with a receptionist.

6. Before signing a lease contract, be sure to review it exhaustively.

   Check the indicated monthly payment, how long the lease is for, what maintenance and repair concerns the landlord will be responsible for, and things like annual rent increases in accordance with inflation.

   You'd also do well to check if there are provisions concerning the possibility of terminating the lease early as well as provisions regarding internet connections, cable service, telephone lines, and other company needs.

   Other important details for you to review include the date of occupancy, right of refusal for the adjoining space, security, and other amenities.

7. Finally, it's a good idea for you to hire a qualified real estate attorney.

   Make sure the attorney specializes in negotiations for leases and that he knows your area.

It's a bonus if he has dealt with the same kind of bridal shop business in the past.

This is important because lease negotiations typically cover hundreds of terms, which makes it a definite advantage to have someone who's gone through it all before on your side.

Managing Your Employees

Once you have your new bridal shop business in place, you'll have to deal with managing your employees, which can be a very tricky process.

If you're not careful, you just might end up babysitting rather than running a successful bridal shop business venture.

This is especially true if a majority of your employees are paid very low hourly rates.

You're lucky if you can hire wonderful employees who don't give you any problems.

However, you'll still have to find effective ways of keeping these wonderful employees in your bridal shop business, and that's where good employee management comes in.

Perhaps the most important aspect of employee management is your ability to set very clear goals and communicate your company objectives very clearly to your employees.

Take note that goal-setting and communicating objectives have to be done regularly.

The more you communicate with your employees in an honest and open manner, the easier it will be for you to manage them.

It's advisable to set monthly, quarterly, and annual goals. And you have to make sure the goals you set are mutual.

This means you should not be forcing your employees to work towards your own goals.

The employees themselves have to believe in those goals and they'll have to be taught how to adjust in case circumstances that keep them from attaining those goals suddenly arise.

Furthermore, you need to realize that goals don't really mean much unless employees' compensations are largely tied up with those goals.

The compensation may be in the form of bonuses, commissions, or salary percentages. What's important is for the employees to have a good motivation for working towards the company's goals.

It's also a good idea to hold a yearly meeting with all of your employees where an annual review will be conducted.

During this review, you should commend your employees for the things they're doing right and discuss solutions for the things that didn't quite work out.

Identifying areas of improvement and finding solutions together can give employees the assurance that they really are part of the company and that they're being valued as individuals, not just as paid workers.

Finally, another very important part of employee management is getting feedback on how YOU are doing at your job.

- How are you as a manager?

- What are you doing right?

- What else can you do to become a better manager?

You have to realize that getting feedback from your employees isn't a waste of your time.

Quite the contrary, in fact.

More often than not, the best ideas for improving a bridal shop business come from the front-liners, as they're usually the ones who know exactly what the customers want.

How to Market Your Bridal Shop Business

Marketing your new bridal shop business probably ranks among the most challenging aspects of putting up a business venture, not to mention that it can also be the most fun.

You should, in fact, be excited about marketing your bridal shop business.

- The main purpose of marketing a bridal shop business is to let your target customers know that you exist and that you have a lot of benefits to offer them.

And take note that the kind of message you convey to your target market is crucial when you market a new bridal shop business.

Branding

Even if you're selling exactly the same item as your closest competitor, you're more likely to come out on top of the competition if you're able to come up with better marketing strategies and if you can successfully create a brand for your company.

Creating a brand for your company will make your bridal shop business more valuable to potential customers.

Regardless of what type of business you're into branding is still important.

In fact, the more you create an attractive personality around your company brand, the more you set yourself apart from the competition, thus giving your bridal shop business a much better opportunity for growth.

How do you know your brand is effective? Simple.

Market it to yourself.

Imagine that you're a would-be customer taking stock of a new player in the industry.

- Does the company brand look, sound, and feel authentic?

- Is it a fun and attractive brand?

Remember that marketing your bridal shop business has to be fun, so don't take it too seriously.

And even while you're working hard to create a brand, you should always remain true to yourself.

That is what will make your brand truly authentic.

And an authentic brand is something your competition can never take away.

Events

Word-of-mouth is still the all-time favourite free marketing method, but you can't really just rely on other people passing on the news about your business to their circle of friends. You'll have to look for other ways of promoting your business in a cost-efficient manner.

One promotional medium that has recently become quite popular among people involved in bridal businesses is known as a bridal event.

In fact, bridal events have become a year-round activity in some places and florists, wedding cake makers, bridal consultants, wedding planners, and many other wedding-related businesses are taking full advantage of the opportunities presented by these events.

Bridal events may just be the perfect venue for you to showcase your own wedding-related products and services.

In promoting your bridal business via bridal events, remember to let your creative juices flow freely.

Don't limit yourself to pitching your products and services; rather, try to catch your target market's attention in creative ways, even without having to make a sales pitch.

Here are some tips on how to optimise the benefits a bridal event has to offer:

1. Set up an exhibit that's sure to catch the interest of your target market. Make good use of colours and contrasts. Again, let your creativity run free!

2. Make your booth attendants wear promotional apparel such as shirts, bags, or caps. You may even consider giving out such apparel or any other type of giveaways to your first 20 booth visitors.

3. Distribute brochures, leaflets, and flyers your prospective clients can browse through for

    future reference. Don't forget to indicate your contact details on these materials.

4. Place your products and/or informational materials in attractive carry bags or takeaway kits.

You may want to check out some companies that offer all types of promotional items you can use in bridal events to make your business stand out from the rest of the event participants.

The best companies even offer discounted rates for bulk orders, so you could really maximise your gains from the marketing strategy you've drawn up.

There's no need to wait.

Sign up for the next bridal event in town and start making your presence felt in the industry.

Business cards

One of the most effective ways for you to let people know of your existence and start building a client base is to hand out creative business cards that are sure to get your target market calling.

Of course, you can't just make any business card and then expect it to work the way you want.

You'll have to make a bit of effort to ensure your business cards deliver the kind of results you expect them to.

Here are some tips on how to prepare effective business cards for your bridal business:

- ✓ Indicate any discounts or special offers you may have at the back of your business card.

    This makes the card more useful to the people you give it to and lets it stand out as a marketing tool.

    While other business cards typically contain nothing more than the name and contact information of a business, yours should contain other information your target market is sure to find useful so they'll be more inclined to call you and hire your services.

- ✓ Use your business card as an attachment to any mail you send out to potential clients.

    Whether you're sending greeting cards, writing a letter, or paying your bills, don't forget to attach your business card.

Remember that just about everyone knows someone who may be planning to get married, so it definitely pays to get your card to as many people as possible.

✓ Whenever you visit your public library, make sure you browse through books related to your bridal business and then leave your business card in each book as a bookmark.

And if you ever borrow library books to read at home, tuck your business card inside each book before returning them.

Chances are good that the next reader will take the card and perhaps pass it on to a family member or friend who's planning to get married. The reader may even keep your card for future reference.

✓ Always bring your business cards wherever you go. You'll never know when you'll get a chance to distribute your card or hand it to someone who needs the kind of products or services you offer.

Keep some of your cards in the office, in your car, in your jacket or shirt pockets, in your wallet, in your bag or briefcase, and at home.

Take note that potential customers for a bridal business can be found just about anywhere, so you should make sure you never miss an opportunity to promote your business.

✓ Hand out two or more cards to each person so he or she can also pass it on to others. This is an excellent way of getting referrals and extending your network.

✓ Many people also appreciate getting more than one card so that when they lose one, they'll still have another card to get your contact details from.

Business cards may just be a small and simple thing, but they can do wonders for your business.

In using this marketing tool, remember to be resourceful, smart, and ready at all times to distribute your cards.

If you're into the bridal business, there can be nothing quite as exciting as assisting the bride-to-be in her wedding preparations.

Somehow, her excitement and happiness just rubs off on you. More often than not, a bride-to-be comes into a bridal shop so full of ideas and visions of colours, dress designs, decorations, and what-not for her big day.

Having a collection of photos of other brides and bridesmaids will definitely be an advantage when you help a bride-to-be arrive at the important decisions concerning her wedding day.

Scrapbooks

There may be times when the bride wants her bridesmaids to wear dresses with the same design, but in different colours.

Seeing what the overall appearance of the ensemble is through photos can help the bride determine if that is really what she wants for her wedding day.

Compiling photos of previous customers and then creating short captions explaining why each "look" worked is a great strategy for helping the client you're currently assisting.

Remember as well that different wedding gown styles and fabrics have a different effect on every woman.

Seeing women with different body types, heights, and complexions will surely help your client decide which dress would look best on her.

Most brides-to-be look through wedding magazines in search of the perfect wedding dress.

This is their way of getting a visual image of how they want their wedding gown to look like. They want to choose from as many different styles as possible to make sure they get the best-looking dress for their big day.

Take your cue from this habit and prepare a number of wedding scrapbooks, taking different budget schedules into consideration.

It can be quite upsetting to finally find the dress of your dreams, only to find out that it's way beyond the ballpark figure of the budget you've set aside for it.

You can save your clients from having to go through this kind of frustration by categorising each of your scrapbooks according to budget.

Make your scrapbooks even more attractive and useful by showing brides in front, side, and back views. This allows you to show off each dress in its entirety and gives your client a better idea of how the dress would look on her.

The same holds true for bridesmaids' dresses, of course.

Different styles and fabrics will naturally look different on different women, so you'd do well to show pictures of them from different sides and angles.

You may also showcase the dresses in different combinations and price ranges in order to provide clients with a wide variety of choices.

Aside from a scrapbook of brides' and bridesmaids' dresses, it's also a good idea to create a book of wedding accessories to help your clients decide if they'll be using a traditional veil, a hat, or any other accessory.

This book will also help the bride decide if she wants a short or long veil to go with her wedding gown.

Create your books in such a way that they guide the bride through the process of sorting out the choices without having to try on any of them yet.

As long as you prepare your book creatively, your photos can very well do the selling for you.

In Conclusion...

If you're serious about making a career out of a bridal business, then you should realise that you'll need to have considerable business and marketing skills.

You should never stop learning new ways of reaching your target market and you should always strive to find inexpensive ways of acquiring new clients.

Among these new and inexpensive strategies is making your presence felt on social media sites, which can be a faster and more effective way to promote your business than any other channel.

So, are you ready to get the ball rolling?

Good luck.

Printed in Great Britain
by Amazon.co.uk, Ltd.,
Marston Gate.